Welcome Home:

The Good News of Jesus

Stephen D Morrison

Printed in the United States of America

Cover photo by Ireen Trummer, modified by the author

www.belovedpublishing.com

www.SDMorrison.org

eBook ISBN: 978-1-63174-153-1

Paperback ISBN: 978-1-63174-152-4

Acknowledgments:

A big thank you goes to everyone who is a part of my Readers Group (the subscribers to my email list). A special shout-out goes to everyone who provided me with valuable feedback on this book. Thank you: Jane Gianoutsos, Adam Garner, John Nankervis, Tim Heath, Wesley Rostoll, Jay Bradley Reed, Lyne Clough, and Fran Means.

I've traveled a lot in my life, especially recently since my wife's been in school. We've lived half in the U.S. and half in Europe these last three years. But it's challenging to live like this, because neither place feels like home anymore. I'm always feeling like an outsider, at least partially, because everything changes so fast when we're gone. Every time we return to either place it's always familiar yet different enough to feel brand new. But never does it feel like coming home, in the traditional sense of the word.

But home isn't a location, I've come to learn. Humans are nomadic by nature; we've always been on the move. Yet to be human is to be in relationship. What are we but the company we keep? We have our individuality, for sure, but would it last without community? Isolation can drive a person insane. Only in community are we free to be individuals; only in relationship are we free to be ourselves.

This is home: community. Home isn't a house you live in, it's the people you share life with. For me that's most of all my wife, but it's also my parents, and my friends from around the globe. My wife is always with me, and thanks to the internet I am only a click away from anyone in the world I want to see. So home for me now is more about these people than it is about what country I happen to be in this month. And it's these people who I love and trust that make up who I am and make up what I call home.

And that's the other thing about home. As a community, home means more than just people, because it's more about being with the people who love you, the people you belong to. It's an often unspoken element to home, but perhaps it's the most essential. Home is when we share life with people we love, who love us, people we'd die for, and who'd die for us. Home is where we can be ourselves without fear, and belong as we are. Home is where we are unconditionally accepted, where we accept unconditionally. Home is an embrace; home is shared laughter. Home is belonging to this kind of community of love.

But does "home" exist? Most of us will spend our entire lives searching for a place like this, a place to be loved, to love, to belong, to be ourselves without fear. But who can say they've ever found it? Even the best people will fail us, fail to embrace us in our shame.

I'm convinced that one of our deepest needs as human beings is belonging. We desire home in a people who will love and accept us unconditionally for who we are. But no one is perfect, we know this. It's okay. People will abandon us, reject us, and fail us, just as we will do the same to other people. We praise the virtues of love and mercy, yet we rarely act in love or mercy, least of all towards ourselves. We are prone to self-hatred and judgement.

"I should be better…"

"I'm so stupid…"

How do we expect to find a home in one another if we're barely even at home with ourselves? Where will we find unconditional love and acceptance if we don't even know how to give it to ourselves?

This is the fatal contradiction of human life: we desire a home we're unfit for. We cannot love unconditionally yet we long to be loved unconditionally. And we know if we can't love like that, no one else can either. No one we ever meet will perfectly be capable of filling our need for unconditional love and acceptance. Our dream of a home where we belong just as we are, without fear, loved and embraced, is an illusion.

Or is it?

What if beyond our humanity there was a community of unconditional love? What if our dream isn't an illusion? What if we desire to belong, to be unconditionally loved, because this place exists and is waiting for us to join in the love? Is the universe so cruel and meaningless that it would give us this desire if it could never be fulfilled? Like a hunger for a food that doesn't

4

exist, a scratch we can never itch, or a thirst we can never quench?

I don't believe so. As the philosopher Immanuel Kant said, "The human heart refuses to believe in a universe without purpose." We have this desire because we have this purpose: to belong, to be loved, to be home. Our hearts will not rest until we find ourselves at peace in this place.

But where is this home, this community of love? And how do we get there? As we've already seen, it cannot be a human home. We can barely love ourselves, how could we ever exist in unconditional love towards one another?

No, this home is beyond our humanity. It transcends our humanity, precedes it, and in a sense prefigures it. This is where we get our ideas of love and acceptance. The pattern of our existence is found here. This is The Great Home, the community of unconditional love which set all love into motion and called all things into being. This community has a name; in common terms, we're talking about God. But not just any God. We're talking about the God who is a community of love, a fellowship of embrace, a dance of acceptance. This community has always been and always will be love.

In other terms we are speaking of what theology has called the Trinity. God in three persons: three persons of love and fellowship who dwell in and with one another in such togetherness that they share one being. This is the community of love, the fellowship called God.

But "God" is a word with far too many connotations behind it. Before I even attempt to tell you how this community of love called God is the home that all humanity desires, I first must be perfectly clear what I mean by this word "God." God is rarely talked about like this. Words like "home" and "community" are far less common in relation to God than words like "holy judge" and "wholly-other." If we're going down this path, the first step involves a deconstruction, a lot of forgetting and leaving behind.

Do me a favor. Drop every preconception you're carrying to the table. You're welcome to

6

pick it all back up on your way out if you'd like, but for now let's start from scratch together.

Who is God?

Whoever "God" is, God has the tendency of looking a lot like us.

Humans are prone to creating God in their own image. We tend to end up with a God who loves what we love and hates what we hate. And in a sense, whenever we speak about God, we are basically "speaking of man in a loud voice," as Karl Barth put it. That's to say, we take our lives and assume that God, whoever that may be, must be like us only perfected and glorified to the nth degree. He must be "super-man," a God of infinite powers and a human face.

"God is tribal. God takes sides." Said Lex Luthor in the 2016 Batman v Superman movie. When God is Superman, a God fashioned in the image of humanity—the "highest good" of mankind—then he's right. Such a God is reduced to a tribal God that takes sides. And for this God it's impossible to be all good and all loving at the same time, because this God has a side to defend and therefore an enemy.

But tribal Gods are illusions of our own making, the result of trying to speak of God by speaking of man in a loud voice.

America has a tribal God. We have a God in love with the American way, in love with our guns, and our capitalism; a God who hates all who oppose America. But so does everyone else. We have all in our societies, even in the subcultures of America, created a God that looks like us. The belt buckles of Nazi soldiers read "Gott mit uns," meaning "God with us." The crusaders of the middle ages famously declared "Deus vult;" "God wills it." Father George Zabelka, a Catholic priest, infamously blessed the atomic bomb in the name of God before it was dropped on Hiroshima and Nagasaki during the August of 1945.

The point? Don't mistake these tribal Gods made in man's image for the true God who is beyond all man-made idols. God is not tribal because God is beyond whatever images mankind has made for God. God is bigger than a tribe.

This is just one of the disastrous mistakes we make whenever we try to understand God in the mirror of mankind. In technical terms, this method is called "natural theology" or "theology from below." But if God is God at all and not a human being, then God cannot be known in this way.

Since Aristotle, philosophy has taught the cognitive principle that "like is only known by like." It's a statement similar to "it takes one to know one," but it differs in allowing for degrees of likeness. This could in one sense mean the degree of similarity is equivalent to the degree of know-ability. In other words, I know my wife because we are alike in many ways, but when she starts talking about her microeconomics homework, I'm lost. I can't know that side of her because I am not like her in that way. "Know" here means knowledge, but more fully understanding, application, and relatability.

The question then is this: Can we know God? Essentially, we cannot, because we are not God and God is not a human being. We cannot know God because even if we were told something about God, that "something" would be far too different from us for us to know what to do with it in our human understanding. Therefore, in this strict sense, God is unknowable to mankind.

But there's an exception. God might be made known to mankind if God were to reveal Godself to us in our language, and therefore from within our humanity itself. We cannot become God to know God, but God might become a man and speak to mankind as a man and reveal God to us.

According to the Christian tradition, this is exactly what has taken place in the person of Jesus Christ. God became a man to make known the ways of God to humanity. God is known only in this way.

If this is true, if God has made Himself known in Jesus Christ, then we can now say who God is and what God is like. But is it true? Has God become a man named Jesus Christ as the Christian tradition professes?

There's no real reason not to think that it's true, for starters. It's an incredibly odd story, and such an odd story seems unlikely to have been made up. In my mind, there are more reasons why this story is plausible then there are reasons it's not.

First of all, it is the only way we could know God at all. Our problem of God's know-ability is nowhere answered better. No other religion in comparison is capable of solving Aristotle's cognitive principle. Therefore, either God is unknowable or God is the Father of Jesus Christ as the Christian tradition professes. If it is true then we can know God, if it is not then God is unknowable entirely.

Second, and personally the most important reason, is the content of Jesus' life. I can't help but see in Jesus the only God worth knowing. And this is the decisive point as we move on. If God is not like Jesus than I don't want anything to do with God at all. When I see Jesus I see a God of love, and therefore the only God worth knowing. When

I see the cross of Jesus I see a suffering God who understands human suffering, and not some abstract deity without emotion. I would not believe in God if it wasn't for Jesus. I don't believe in God as an abstract principle of existence; I believe concretely in the God and Father of Jesus Christ. It's for Christ's sake I believe.

For me I find more compelling evidence in Jesus Christ than anywhere else that God is for me, God is with me, and God loves me. In brief these are the three things I want to expound about what God is like in the light of Jesus.

God is with us. God with us does not mean yet another tribal God, but that God is with all humanity. God is in solidarity with the human race, with us in all our fears, sorrows, disasters, and our joys as well. In Jesus we have a brother who knows us, understands us, and has joined us where we are.

God is for us. What God has done for the human race in Jesus Christ was done in our favor. God acts not in opposition to humanity, but always for us, with our benefit in mind. In the person and work of Jesus Christ this has been made clear. God is the one from whom we can expect good and only good.

God is love. This is the final and most important point. We say that God *is* love, not that God *loves,* because God in Godself is a fellowship. This returns our discussion to God as a community of love, as our home, as the place we belong to. God is not isolated in Godself, lonely for all eternity. Through Jesus we discover that God is a Father, a Son, and a Spirit. Jesus constantly referred both to His Father and to His Spirit during His life and ministry. These persons exist in a mutual fellowship of love and shared life. This is why God is love: God in Godself is this love affair of one being joined inseparably by the shared love of the Father, Son, and Spirit. In short, God is a relationship. God is in Godself a community of love.

Now that we've returned to this concept of home, the community of love, we must also return to our situation as a human race. We may say,

"Good for God to have such a nice community of love," but we know we will never belong there with our imperfect love and our failed mercy.

But what if God were to open His life up to us so that we might join Him where He is in his fellowship of love? Yet how could we accept and join God there, with the infinite distance between God and man? How could we, in our feeble inadequacy, take part in the life of God?

What Happened at Christmas?

God came to humanity. God became a man like all men, bone of our bone and flesh of our flesh. God in humility came low to meet us where we are. It was not left to us to reach out to God, God reached us. While we were lost in our darkness, God came to us as our light.

This is the message of Christmas. God did not will to be God without us. God willed to be our God, to be next to us and one of us, and in Christ God became this God. God became a man in all its fullness. He became a man yet remained God. Because Jesus Christ is God who became a man while remaining God, God can free mankind (all mankind) from death and destruction. Because God became a man, mankind can be reconciled to God.

In the previous section God became man to reveal God to us. Following this, we now are saying that God became a man to save and heal mankind. The bible uses the terms light and darkness in connection with Jesus and the world

15

He entered. Jesus Christ is the light in our darkness, illuminating our darkness and overcoming it. Illumination makes known; Christ came to reveal God. Yet light also extinguishes darkness by overcoming it; Christ came to save and heal.

What does Jesus save us from? In short, from ourselves. But without Christ illuminating our darkness we would never have known what sin is or the state of our diseased condition. We know something is wrong, but before Christ saved us we didn't know what it was. In the light of Christ's salvation, we know the seriousness of our sin and our condition which He has overcome. Sin is known only in this way, not before salvation but after it. This is what the bible calls our sin and our sinful nature, it is our pride, and our brokenness. This is what we are saved from, made known in the light of Christ's redemption.

Jesus rescues us and reconciles us to God. God does not will to be God without us, and therefore Jesus Christ entered into our darkness to bring us home where we belong in the embrace of the Triune God of love.

But how does God do this?

We'll examine two important ways in which Christ affects us in His life. We will examine both the passive and the active way He saves and heals.

Passively, God in Christ heals our broken humanity by assuming it as His own; God becomes a man. While a doctor may treat a patient by standing above him, working from the outside, giving advice on how to get better, God heals by becoming the patient. God does not solve the problem of human sin by standing above us. God heals our sin by taking it up as His own, by assuming the very same diseased humanity. The early church father Gregory Nazianzen would say it like this: "The unassumed is the unhealed." And the converse of that statement means that what Christ has become He has healed. This is how Jesus Christ heals our broken humanity.

Actively, God in Christ saves by taking up our cause as His own. What is our cause? It is our ascent to God, all our attempts of being faithful to

God, trying to serve God, and obey God. But we have failed, each and every one of us. We are not righteous; we are full of pride. We are unable to reach God on the strength of our morality or our religiosity. None of it has ever succeeded. But God came to man, to lift us out of our condition, out of our sin and mess, and into His loving embrace. Jesus Christ fulfilled the response of man to God as both a truly faithful God to man and a truly faithful man to God. He upheld God's faithfulness to us and, in our place, He was faithful to God as a man. Jesus Christ found us in our lost-ness and brought us back home where we belong, carrying us all up on His shoulders. This is how Jesus Christ saves our humanity from the sin of a prideful and fallen condition.

God has not left a single step of our journey home up to us. In Christ, God has humbled Himself to our level and healed us and set us free to bring us home to the embrace of the Triune God. God has reached us. He participated in our life so that we might participate in His.

But what if we, brought home to this embrace, find that we love imperfectly, or sin and fail God? Though we've been brought home, will we get thrown out as soon as we prove how unworthy we are of this fellowship? Or in this way will we only ever belong superficially, as a show but not in the actuality of who we are? How will we ever *truly* belong in the life of God?

What Happened at Easter?

Love is not sentiment, especially not for God. Love is not what we've mass-produced in Hollywood, a feel-good emotion, a good idea— even the best of ideas. Love is action. For God, love gives, love empties itself for another, love sacrifices. When the bible says that God loved the world in the very next breath it says "He gave." God gives mankind the greatest good, Himself. When God says "I love you" He lays down all that He is for your sake. This is the message of Easter: God loves the world more than He loves Himself; God loves *you* more than He loves Himself.

Our problem is that we're unworthy, we love imperfectly, we live pride-fully and selfishly. We finished the last section with this. Even if Jesus Christ has brought us home to the embrace of His Father in the Spirit's love, how can we, selfish and proud people, ever truly belong there in perfect love? When we fail to love perfectly will this community of love accept us as one of their own? Of course love will accept us, it's what perfect love does, but will we really belong here in the unconditional love of God?

We have the problem of us. (I have the problem of me.) If we have any chance at life in the Triune love of God we must be made new. The old must be put away.

Jesus Christ took up our cause as a man. On the cross Jesus carried our condition and completed our cause. It was not enough, we have seen, for us to be forgiven or even brought home. Forgiveness may let us off the hook and set our minds at ease, but we remain in our darkness, in our sinful condition. God must not only forgive us to have us home, truly free and embraced there; God must destroy our darkness. God must remove and undo our fallen condition, he must put us to death.

How else? Since the sin and the sinner are inseparable? We are not merely what we do, but what we do is who we are. We not only love imperfectly; we are imperfect. We not only act prideful; we are proud. We are sinners.

But how is God to love us and in the same breath stand opposed to our diseased condition?

How will God show favor on us while we remain in our sinful state?

God determined to act in our favor, to be our God unrelenting in His love for us. On the cross, God acted in self-sacrifice. God revealed Himself to be the God who loves us more than He loves Himself. This is how God solves the dilemma of our human condition: God dies for us, as us, instead of us.

But the crucifixion of Jesus is at once an act of God's mercy towards mankind, and a pronouncement of judgement against our condition. Think of it like this:

When I forgive you, in that forgiveness there is mercy and there is judgement. Because although I accept you and embrace you, I am still taking your wrongs seriously. I forgive them in mercy, but the wrong done is still judged as wrong. But this judgement comes only in and with this mercy. By forgiving you I am not saying that what you have done is no longer wrong. I still judge your mistake as a mistake. But mercy triumphs over judgement, and I forgive despite the wrong done. This is how God forgives and redeems us. This is how the cross is at once mercy and judgement.

Yet, the stunning event of the crucifixion goes far beyond forgiveness and mercy. Because in mercy God judges our condition, God must also remove our sinful condition. As such, the cross is an act of judgement, but here's the astonishing thing: it is not our judgement. On the cross God did not judge mankind. On the cross God judged Himself, in our place! It was a judgement that we deserved, and in this sense it was our judgement. Yet God took it upon Himself. As Karl Barth puts it, "The passion of Jesus Christ is the judgement of God in which the Judge Himself was the judged."

God has revealed on the cross that He loves us more than He loves Himself, and because of this, in outrageous mercy and grace, the Son of God has taken our judgement as His own. The Judge is judged in our place, thereby destroying our sin in the flesh.

This is how God overcomes our diseased humanity: He annihilates it in Himself as the judged Judge who suffers the judgement and death incurred by our human condition. He takes our cause in becoming a man and He sees it all the way through to the bitter end. He assumes our fallen condition and destroys it in His death. As Robert Capon once said, the death of Jesus is like a "black hole" in which our diseased humanity has been lost forever. Jesus dies our death. He suffers our sinful condition. He dies *as us*, as a human being in our flesh, to undo our suffering in His death and set us free.

In order for the human race to find itself once again home and healed in the embrace of the Triune God, in the love of the Father, Son, and Spirit where we belong, God must take up our cause and remove our old, diseased condition entirely. The forgiveness of sins would not be enough, and it was never the point. Forgiveness is not the end of atonement; it is the means to the end. God must undo our corruption at its root, not merely forgive us. And He has done exactly that by dying the death we deserve in our flesh. The end of atonement is our adoption and inclusion into the life of God. To stop at forgiveness would be to stop short of the gospel. Forgiveness is a part of the gospel, but not the central point. The central point is our adoption as sons and daughters of God.

We have died with Christ; our sin nature was crucified on that cross with Him. And in the grave our diseased humanity, our old nature, was lost forever. As Paul writes, "I have been crucified with Christ." (Gal. 2:20) And elsewhere, "…one died for all, therefore all died." (1 Cor. 5:14) When Jesus died, you died. The death of Jesus is the annihilation of our diseased human condition once and for all. As Paul continues to say, "Therefore if anyone is in Christ, he is a new creation; the old things passed away: behold, new things have come." (2 Cor. 5:17)

When Jesus died you died with Him. You died in your mess and insecurity, you died in your sin and failure, you died in your mistakes and darkness. But in the resurrection, Jesus burst forth and gave you new life, as a new creation. In His death our old nature has met its end, and in His resurrection we are new.

The resurrection and ascension of Jesus Christ are the fulfillment of God's will for us. He took up our cause so completely that He did not leave us as we were. He did not stop with the death of Jesus as our death to sin, but re-created the core of our nature in His resurrection. We are in Christ and share in His nature, as "partakers of the Divine nature." (2 Pet. 1:4) He has taken hold of our existence, healed our brokenness, destroyed our diseased condition, and raised us to new life. He has brought us home to His Father. He has seated us in heavenly places. We are included in the center of the Trinitarian life of love and acceptance where we belong. Jesus has taken hold of us, lifted us up from out of our darkness. He has made us new, and finally, He has brought us home.

We are a new creation in Christ, and now nothing stands between us and fellowship in God's community of love. We have nothing to fear, we can be ourselves fully and without reserve because we will always be accepted in this fellowship. This is how God made a way for us to belong to Him, not superficially, but truly to belong in His fellowship.

But there are still a lot of questions left unanswered. If this is what has objectively happened for us in Jesus Christ, how do we subjectively experience it? How do we live in this community, and what do we do with all the contradictions we experience in this life? In short, how do we live today in this community while at once we live in this world?

Welcome Home

We belong to the Triune God of endless love, boundless acceptance, and radical grace. We are home here. God willed from before all time in Jesus Christ that you would be included in this community of life, joy, and love. In time Jesus Christ has made God's will a reality. We are home. Our mistakes are overcome and we are free for this fellowship. We've been adopted into the community of God's love. God has always loved us and willed for us to be here, and the good news of Jesus is that now we are here, we are home in Him. Welcome home.

But…

This is where we have to begin looking at two further sides of the good news which clarify what I'm saying here. First, the subjective side, because what good is all this if were not affected by it personally? And second, the side of hope, because while this is true it is still on the way to full manifestation in our life and world.

Jesus is God's command to open our eyes and see that we are home in the loving embrace of the Father, Son, and Spirit. Faith is the subjective side of the good news. Faith sees. Faith is the awakening power of the Holy Spirit to see the reality already accomplished in Jesus Christ. As such, faith is cognitive in character and not redemptive. Faith sees redemption; faith does not redeem. Faith is not what we do to earn a life of fellowship with God; faith is the awakening power of the Holy Spirit to see we already have it. Accordingly, faith is a gift. But faith is also a human act of obedience, the decision to recognize the reconciliation of the world to God in Jesus Christ.

The object of faith is Jesus Christ. Jesus is what faith believes, what faith trusts. Faith rises and falls in relation to Jesus. It is in relation to Jesus that faith is faith at all. In this sense, faith is strictly faith in Jesus Christ, not some abstract principle of belief. Faith is based on Jesus, upheld by Jesus.

In a picture, imagine a father and his child walking down the street hand in hand. Who's holding whose hand? Is the child holding together the grasp of their hands? Certainly not. The father is more responsible and able to hold onto his child's hand. Though the child holds onto him, it is ultimately the father who holds onto his child. This is faith. God is faithful to us, He holds our hand. Our response is faith: our feeble attempt to hold onto the hand holding onto us. Faith is based not on our ability to see or hold onto God's faithfulness in Jesus Christ. Faith is our meager response to the faithfulness of God in Christ, awakening us and holding onto us. We do act in holding on, but the important element in faith is that God is holding onto us, walking with us, awakening us in freedom to see what He has done in Jesus. Faith is first the faithfulness of God towards us, and only second is it our response.

This is the subjective side of the good news. We let the Spirit awaken us to freedom in the community of God's love, to see, to acknowledge, recognize, and confess, what Jesus has done to bring us home.

In another picture, imagine you are at a grand festival, the grandest you can picture, with delicious food, beautiful music, and plenty of dancing and laughter. You have a choice. You are already here at the party, the festivities are in full swing and you are invited to join in, but will you sulk or celebrate? Will you feast, dance, laugh, and enjoy yourself, or will you sit in the corner ignoring the party entirely?

This too is faith. Faith is cognitive. You are already included in the fellowship of God's love, the grand festival, but will you open your eyes and see it? Will you celebrate it? Will you live loved, unashamed, and free because you are loved, forgiven, and set free? Will you belong and let yourself rest in the grace of the God who loves you unconditionally? Will you let go of all your past mistakes and what you used to be, and embrace who you have become in Jesus? Will you forgive yourself and love yourself as you have been forgiven and loved? Will you see yourself as a child of God belonging to the family of love? Will you define yourself radically as this beloved, because it is the deepest truth of your existence? Will you forget every voice of rejection and every time you felt inadequate? Will you be here, will you be home, where you belong, where you have always belonged? Will you look up to see the smiling face of your Father God, receive the warm embrace of your brother Jesus, and hear the joyful laugh of the Holy Spirit? Will you dance in the love of the Father, the friendship of Jesus, and the hope of the Spirit? Will you be here, be home? Welcome home.

But you are not alone here. You have many brothers and sisters in this faith. Faith is also a community. This community is called the church. However dysfunctional or misguided it may seem, you belong here too. We belong to God but also to each other. God has reconciled the world to Himself, and also the world *to* itself. We are the community of faith learning to live life together. We are learning what it means to be the beloved of God, and to love like God loves; to follow Jesus by loving our neighbor, and making friends with our enemies; to practice peace, and serve the poor.

This is the horizontal element which corresponds to the vertical element of faith. This is the church and the body of Jesus Christ.

And now we have to turn to our second consideration: hope. The gospel of Jesus Christ proclaims a finished work of the world reconciled to God. But it is not yet a work of totality; the world is not yet redeemed. We stand between the wedding vows and the consummation. Christ has completed the work, and in His life, death, and resurrection we see prefigured the redemption of the whole world which is still to come. This is our hope. We live in the expectation that what God has done in Jesus Christ He will one day do for the whole creation.

The world will be made new. The dead will raise, and death will be no more. Death will die, and the grave will be overcome for good. All creation, the whole cosmos, will be a new creation. There will be a new heaven and a new earth, and we will live forever in the embrace of God and each other. Heaven and earth will be one, and God will manifest His glory for all the world to see. Then every eye will see and every tongue will confess that Jesus Christ is Lord. We live in hopeful expectation for this glorious new beginning.

When Jesus rose again He rose as the first fruits of this new creation. In Him the cosmic rebirth of all things is promised and prefigured. He rose again in the power of the Spirit and by the will of the Father, because one day the whole world will be made new and share in His new life. This is our hope.

But this also adds a degree of "now but not yet" to everything we have said here. It is completely true that we are made new in Jesus, but it is also true that one day the fullness of that newness will be unveiled. It is completely true that we are saved, healed, and set free in Christ, but it is also true that this will be fully manifest in the age to come. We have the fullness of our adoption and salvation now, but we see through a veil. One day the veil will be removed and we will see more fully the fullness of what Jesus Christ has done.

We live as people "on the way." We therefore live by hope. We live in the hope that Jesus Christ will return and God will make all things new. We live with the expectation that what has happened in Jesus' resurrection from the dead will happen for the whole creation on a cosmic scale.

But while we live in the now and hope for the not yet, still we have this life to live in the love of God and the joy of the Holy Spirit. We are not alone. We have the Spirit in us as the down payment of what's to come (2 Cor.1:22). So we live our lives in expectation and we live in fellowship with God and each other. But we live.

The Spirit of God with us is the affirmation of life in this moment. God's Spirit is the Spirit of life. As we affirm life and love life, life in the now becomes life worth living. We may be people on the way with hopeful hearts set on the future, but this does not steal away from today. Instead, hope for the future gives meaning to life. Without hope life would lose its meaning, but with renewed hope we more fully embrace our lives in the present.

Furthermore, the hope of a new creation means that nothing in the end is lost or forgotten. Whatever we do in this life, be it loving our children, serving the poor, fighting injustice, painting a landscape, writing poetry, or working faithfully at our jobs—it will all last into God's future. We're not left to live this life in waiting without purpose. We get to work towards God's future and ours, to build something with our lives that will last into the Kingdom of God and the new creation.

We are loved in this life, we are a part of God's community of love and acceptance. We have been included into the love of the Triune God, and as we live lives loved and affirmed by God's Spirit, we wait in expectation and hope for the redemption of the cosmos. We are home and we are going home.

Welcome home.

Some Scriptures Considered

For further clarification and biblical support. All scripture quotations are from the English Standard Version (ESV).

Ephesians 1:5-6

"In love he predestined us for adoption as sons through Jesus Christ, according to the purpose of his will, to the praise of his glorious grace, with which he has blessed us in the Beloved."

God's will is Jesus Christ. From before all-time God desired to adopt many sons and daughters in the son-ship of Jesus. In time this is what Christ has accomplished: adoption. Just as Jesus is first and originally the Son of His Father, so God's will for humanity is first and originally adoption. Above justification, reconciliation, and even atonement this is what God had in mind for the human race. All these are a means to an end with that end being our adoption as sons and daughters of God in Jesus Christ. A central place has been given to our adoption throughout this book for this reason. The title *Welcome Home* is itself an illusion to the prodigal son story of Luke 15, which speaks of a son returning home to his father's open arms.

2 Corinthians 13:14

"The grace of the Lord Jesus Christ and the love of God and the fellowship of the Holy Spirit be with you all."

God is a fellowship: three persons, one being. I have followed what's known as the "social" doctrine of the Trinity here, as opposed to the more traditional approach. In the social doctrine of the Trinity the emphasis is on the three persons united in love, rather than the one being in three forms. Thus, I have used terms like "community," "relationship," and "fellowship" to describe the Father, Son, and Holy Spirit. This I believe best portrays the biblical witness to God, especially in the event of the crucifixion. (For more see the work of Jürgen Moltmann, specifically *The Trinity and the Kingdom*, for an exposition of the social Trinity.)

John 1:1-2; 14

"In the beginning was the Word, and the Word was with God, and the Word was God. He was in the beginning with God. …And the Word became flesh and dwelt among us, and we have seen his glory, glory as of the only Son from the Father, full of grace and truth."

With these first lines John makes a clear distinction within God, that within the one God there is diversity. (I.e., that God is a Trinity.) This is one of the best examples of the Trinity in scripture. And then the Word, the logos, the reason, became flesh. This emphasizes what we've said in section two. We cannot know God unless the Word became flesh. But since the Word that became flesh is Jesus Christ, we can know God by looking to Jesus.

Philippians 2:5-11

"Have this mind among yourselves, which is
yours in Christ Jesus, who, though he was in the
form of God, did not count equality with God a
thing to be grasped, but emptied himself, by
taking the form of a servant, being born in the
likeness of men. And being found in human
form, he humbled himself by becoming obedient
to the point of death, even death on a cross.
Therefore God has highly exalted him and
bestowed on him the name that is above every
name, so that at the name of Jesus every knee
should bow, in heaven and on earth and under
the earth, and every tongue confess that Jesus
Christ is Lord, to the glory of God the Father."

Jesus Christ in absolute humility and grace
stooped low and became what we are. He
"emptied Himself," and was born in the likeness
of fallen humanity. He humbled Himself to such a
tremendous end for our sakes. This is what God is
like. God in His freedom is the God who can be

self-limited and weak and fragile, subject to death and suffering, all for our sakes. In Christ God has declared Himself to be our God, the God of mankind, a human God. He is the God that does not will to be God without us. He is not only the God on high, but has become in Christ the God of our suffering, the God of humanity. This is how God is glorified: He becomes small and weak, in radical humility, for our sake, for you and for me.

2 Corinthians 8:9

"For you know the grace of our Lord Jesus Christ, that though he was rich, yet for your sake he became poor, so that you by his poverty might become rich."

God became poor, took upon Himself our bankrupt condition, to lift up our condition into the richness of His life. He came for our sakes, not for any benefit of his own. God bankrupt Himself, risking His very existence as God by entering into an anti-God world, our world of sin, and He reconciled us back to Himself in the world of His

Father. He entered the far country to bring us home. He risked everything for our sakes, setting aside the grandeur of his nature for our frail existence.

Romans 8:3-4

"For God has done what the law, weakened by the flesh, could not do. By sending his own Son in the likeness of sinful flesh and for sin, he condemned sin in the flesh, in order that the righteous requirement of the law might be fulfilled in us, who walk not according to the flesh but according to the Spirit."

This shows the utter seriousness of our condition, and the depths Christ went to for our sake. It also shows what our real problem has always been. It's not that we broke the rules or merely sinned, but that sin corrupted our very nature. We are thoroughly sinners. In order for Christ to rescue us He must personally intervene, He must assume our sinful condition and condemn sin in the flesh. This verse shows how serious sin must be if God went to such lengths in Christ to destroy it. And it also shows the active side of Christ's incarnation, that Jesus not only healed us by assumption, but took up our cause and fulfilled the covenant as a man in our place.

Galatians 2:19-20

"For through the law I died to the law, so that I might live to God. I have been crucified with Christ. It is no longer I who live, but Christ who lives in me. And the life I now live in the flesh I live by faith in the Son of God, who loved me and gave himself for me."

When we imagine the cross of Jesus, we cannot imagine ourselves as mere spectators. We were there hanging on that cross with Jesus Christ. We were crucified, we died there with Christ, and our old nature was buried and forgotten for good. God took our sinful flesh and removed it in the death of Jesus.

2 Corinthians 5:14-19

"For the love of Christ controls us, because we have concluded this: that one has died for all, therefore all have died; and he died for all, that those who live might no longer live for themselves but for him who for their sake died and was raised. From now on, therefore, we regard no one according to the flesh. Even though we once regarded Christ according to the flesh, we regard him thus no longer. Therefore, if anyone is in Christ, he is a new creation. The old has passed away; behold, the new has come. All this is from God, who through Christ reconciled us to himself and gave us the ministry of reconciliation; that is, in Christ God was reconciling the world to himself, not counting their trespasses against them, and entrusting to us the message of reconciliation."

All humanity was on that cross with Jesus. God was in Christ reconciling *the world* to Himself. Not only were you and I on that cross, co-crucified with Christ, and not only where the Christians or the good people on that cross; truly all creation was crucified with Christ. He took hold of our fearful existence, our corruption, and He destroyed it in His death. We all died with Him. The old creation was put aside in Christ's death, and we await with expectation the new creation of all things to be unveiled, that which began at Christ's resurrection.

Colossians 2:11-15

"In him also you were circumcised with a circumcision made without hands, by putting off the body of the flesh, by the circumcision of Christ, having been buried with him in baptism, in which you were also raised with him through faith in the powerful working of God, who raised him from the dead. And you, who were dead in your trespasses and the uncircumcision of your flesh, God made alive together with him, having forgiven us all our trespasses, by canceling the record of debt that stood against us with its legal demands. This he set aside, nailing it to the cross. He disarmed the rulers and authorities and put them to open shame, by triumphing over them in him."

This is how God saves: God overcomes sin through suffering; God is victorious over death by dying. We have overcome in Him through His victory over sin and death. Our old man has been laid aside and we share in the life of Christ. We are set free in Him.

Romans 8:1-5, 15

"There is therefore now no condemnation for those who are in Christ Jesus. For the law of the Spirit of life has set you free in Christ Jesus from the law of sin and death. For God has done what the law, weakened by the flesh, could not do. By sending his own Son in the likeness of sinful flesh and for sin, he condemned sin in the flesh, in order that the righteous requirement of the law might be fulfilled in us, who walk not according to the flesh but according to the Spirit. For those who live according to the flesh set their minds on

the things of the flesh, but those who live
according to the Spirit set their minds on the
things of the Spirit. … For you did not receive
the spirit of slavery to fall back into fear, but you
have received the Spirit of adoption as sons, by
whom we cry, 'Abba! Father!'"

We cry "Abba, dear Father!" because we truly
have been included in the life of God, we truly are
the sons and daughters of God. We stand as we
are, vulnerable and raw, without any illusions
about ourselves, and we are accepted just this
way, as we truly are. We have nothing to fear. We
are home.

Colossians 3:3-4
"For you have died, and your life is hidden with
Christ in God. When Christ who is your life
appears, then you also will appear with him in
glory."

Our life is hidden in Jesus. On the last day when He is revealed, so we will see who we've been made in Him. We are a new creation in Him. We are this right now, but soon the veil will be lifted and all will see. This is the new creation of the world which is to come, prefigured in Christ's resurrection, and this is our hope.

Afterword

I have attempted in this book to make a clear, concise, and simple exposition of the good news of Jesus Christ, the Son of the Father, who in the power of the Holy Spirit has rescued the human race from sin and darkness, making us new and giving us hope for the future. However successful I have been I owe entirely to this God who has loved me so, who is so gracious towards me in all things, even in allowing me to write this little book.

My hope, above all else, is that the God of the gospel is glorified in this book. Far too often the gospel dishonors God in being more about what we must do to get on His good side—As if God in Christ hasn't already accomplish everything for our salvation! —than it is about what has taken place for the world in Jesus Christ. God saves us single-handedly. This is the good news of Jesus. It's not the message of a God out to get you unless you join a religion or pray the right prayer or get your act together. It's the best news you've ever heard, that God accepts you and embraces you in spite of all that, in spite of your mess, in spite of your failures, in spite of the fact you haven't been to church in years. God doesn't care about what you haven't done or promised to do but never do or whatever your moral sins are, God just cares about you. And in Jesus Christ He has done whatever's necessary to prove it.

You may have questions, you may not "get" everything, life still might not make sense (when will it ever?), but my hope is after reading this book you'll come away with the knowledge that you are cared about. God is for you. God loves you. God is love from before all time and He has included you in that love, in the dance of the Father, Son, and Holy Spirit. Be there, be in that love. Accept love, accept forgiveness, accept God's open arms.

In the quiet of this moment you just may sense the presence of mystery, the presence of the unknown. Don't ignore it, embrace it. God is with you. If you listen you just might hear a whisper of

His love for you. The Grand Festival is all around you and it's time to join the fun. Welcome home.

Stephen D Morrison

About the Author:

Stephen D. Morrison is a young, creative writer of theology and fiction. He is happily married to the love of his life, Ketlin. Together they live in between the United States and Tallinn, Estonia. Stephen is the author of several books including *We Belong: Trinitarian Good News* and *10 Reasons Why the Rapture Must Be Left Behind.* To learn more about Stephen, as well as to stay up to date about his latest work, please visit his website:

www.SDMorrison.org

Further Reading

Compiled here is a list of books and articles for further reading on the subject of the gospel, as well as the other subjects that were brought up in this book.

Books:

Athanasius, St.:

On The Incarnation

Barth, Karl:

Church Dogmatics II.2 and IV.1

Deliverance to the Captives

Dogmatics in Outline

Capon, Robert:

Between Noon and Three

Kingdom, Grace, Judgement

Kruger, C. Baxter:

Jesus and the Undoing of Adam

The Great Dance

The Shack Revisited

Moltmann, Jürgen:

Jesus Christ for Today's World

The Living God and the Fullness of Life

The Trinity and the Kingdom

Morrison, Stephen D:

We Belong: Trinitarian Good News

Torrance, James B:

Worship, Community and the Triune God of Grace

Torrance, Thomas F:

Atonement: The Person and Work of Christ

Incarnation: The Person and Life of Christ

Preaching Christ Today

The Doctrine of God

Articles:

Morrison, Stephen D:

"8 Brilliant Karl Barth Quotes on Atonement (CD IV.1 Summarized)" - http://www.sdmorrison.org/8-brilliant-karl-barth-quotes-on-atonement-cd-iv-1-summarized/

"8 Incredible Karl Barth Quotes (CD II.2

Summarized)" - http://www.sdmorrison.org/8-incredible-karl-barth-quotes/

"I Know Someone Who Was in Hell: Christ (Moltmann)" - http://www.sdmorrison.org/i-know-someone-who-was-in-hell-christ-moltmann/

"Jesus Christ: The Future of Mankind" - http://www.sdmorrison.org/jesus-christ-the-future-of-mankind/

"Karl Barth's Doctrine of Faith in CD IV.1" - http://www.sdmorrison.org/karl-barths-doctrine-faith-cd-iv-1/

"Karl Barth's Revolutionary Doctrine of Sin" - http://www.sdmorrison.org/karl-barth-s-revolutionary-doctrine-of-sin/

"Not One - Good Friday Meditation" - http://www.sdmorrison.org/not-one-good-friday-meditation/

"What is Election? (A Summary)" - http://www.sdmorrison.org/what-is-election-a-summary/

Other Voices

Collected quotes to further support and clarify the good news of Jesus Christ.

St. Athanasius of Alexandria:

"Thus, taking a body like our own... liable to the corruption of death, He surrendered His body to death instead of all, and offered it to the Father. This He did out of sheer love for us, so that in His death all might die, and the law of death thereby be abolished... This He did that He might turn again to incorruption men who had turned back to corruption, and make them alive through death by the appropriation of His body and by the grace of His resurrection. Thus He would make death to disappear from them as utterly as straw from fire. The Word perceived that corruption could not be gotten rid of otherwise than through death." (*On the Incarnation*. Sections 8-9)

"For by the sacrifice of His own body He did two things: He put an end to the law of death which barred our way; and He made a new beginning of life for us, by giving us the hope of resurrection." (*Ibid.* Section 10)

St. Hilary of Poitiers:

"He by Whom man was made had nothing to gain by becoming Man; it was our gain that God was incarnate and dwelt among us, making all flesh His home by taking upon Him the flesh of One. We were raised because He was lowered; shame to Him was glory to us. He, being God, made flesh His residence, and we in return are lifted anew from the flesh to God." (*On the Trinity*, 1.25)

"He conquered death, broke the gates of hell, won for Himself a people to be His co-heirs, lifted fleshed from corruption up to the glory of eternity." (*Ibid.*)

St. Irenaeus of Lyons:

"For it was for this end that the Word of God was made man, and He who was the Son of God became the Son of man, that man, having been taken into the Word, and receiving the adoption, might become the son of God. For by no other means could we have attained to incorruptibility and immortality, unless we had been united to incorruptibility and immortality. But how could we be joined to incorruptibility and immortality, unless, first, incorruptibility and immortality had become that which we also are, so that the corruptible might be swallowed up by incorruptibility, and the mortal by immortality, that might receive the adoption of sons?" (*Against Heresies* Book III 19.1)

John McLeod Campbell:

"The atonement is the development of the incarnation." (*The Nature of Atonement*, p. 229, Handsel Press, 1996)

"[Jesus] is the revealer of God to man [and] also the revealer of man to himself. Apart from Christ we know not our God, and apart from Christ we know not ourselves." (*Ibid.* p. 136)

Thomas F. Torrance:

"He [Jesus] was so one with us that when he died we died, for he did not die for himself but for us, and he did not die alone, but we died in him as those whom he had bound to himself inseparably by his incarnation. Therefore when he rose again we rose in him and with him, and when he presented himself before the face of the Father, he presented us also before God, so that we are already accepted of God in him once and for all." (*Atonement: The Person and Work of Christ*, p. 152, InterVarsity Press, 2009)

"He made our lost and damned condition, our death under divine judgement, his very own. ... In the incarnation and the cross Christ has penetrated into the darkest depths of our abject human misery and perdition, where he takes our place, intercedes for us, substitutes himself for us, and makes the atoning restitution which we could not make, thereby reconciling us to God." (*Preaching Christ Today*, p. 30, Eerdmans, 1994)

"In far too much preaching of Christ the ultimate responsibility is taken off the shoulders of the Lamb of God and put upon the shoulders of the poor sinner, and he knows well in his heart that he cannot cope with it." (*Ibid.* p. 35)

"There is no unknown God behind the back of Jesus for us to fear, to see the Lord Jesus is to see the very face of God." (*Ibid.* p. 55)

James B. Torrance:

"Christ does not heal us as an ordinary doctor might, by standing over us, diagnosing our sickness, prescribing medicine for us to take and then going away, leaving us to get better as we follow His instructions. No, he becomes the patient. He assumes that very humanity which is in need of redemption, and by being anointed by the Spirit in our humanity, by a life of perfect obedience, by dying and rising again, for us, our humanity is healed in Him, in His person. We are not just healed in Him, in His person. We are not just healed through Christ, because of the work of Christ, but in and through Christ. Person and work must not be separated." (*Worship, Community and the Triune Grace of God*, p. 53, InterVarsity Press, 1996)

"He lifts us up out of ourselves to participate in the very life and communion of the Godhead, that life of communion for which we were created." (*Ibid.* p. 22)

"The prime purpose of the incarnation, in the love of God, is to lift us up into the life of communion, of participation in the very Triune life of God." (*Ibid.* p. 32)

C. Baxter Kruger:

"The Christian God is interested in relationship with us, and not just relationship, but union, and not just union, but such a union that everything He is and has—all glory and fullness, all joy and beauty and unbridled life—is to be shared with us and to become as much ours as it is His. The plan from the beginning, in the Christian vision, is that God would give Himself to us, and nothing less, so that we could be filled to overflowing with the divine life." (*Jesus and the Undoing of Adam*, Perichoresis Press, 2007)

"The gospel is the good news of what became of the Son of God, and of what became of us in him. It is the news that Adam and all of us were crucified with Christ, dead and buried, and on the third day Adam and all of us were quickened with new life and raised with Jesus, and then lifted up to the Father's right hand in Jesus' ascension and seated with Christ." (*Ibid.*)

"To my mind, the central passion of the human heart is to be filled with the great dance, and the chief and maddening riddle of human life is to understand what the dance is and how to live in it." (*The Great Dance: The Christian Vision Revisited*, Kindle Locations 161-163, Perichoresis Press.)

C. S. Lewis:

"In Christianity God is not a static thing— not even a person—but a dynamic, pulsating activity, a life, almost a kind of drama. Almost, if you will not find me irrelevant, a kind of dance." (*Mere Christianity* p. 152, Macmillan, 1952)

"In the Incarnation God the Son takes the body and human soul of Jesus, and, through that, the whole environment of Nature, all the creaturely predicament, into His own being. So that 'He came down from Heaven' can almost be transposed into 'Heaven drew earth up into it,' and locality, limitation, sleep, sweat, footsore weariness, frustration, pain, doubt, and death, are, from before all worlds, known by God from within. The pure light walks the earth; the darkness, received into the heart of Deity, is there swallowed up. Where, except in uncreated light, can the darkness be drowned?" (*Letters to Malcolm* p. 71, Mariner Books, 2002)

"It would seem that Our Lord finds our desires, not too strong, but too weak. We are half-hearted creatures, fooling about with drink and sex and ambition when infinite joy is offered us, like an ignorant child who wants to go on making mud pies in a slum because he cannot imagine what is meant by the offer of a holiday at the sea. We are far too easily pleased." (*The Weight of Glory*, Harper One, 2001)

Robert Capon:

"...Grace cannot prevail until law is dead, until moralizing is out of the game. ...until our fatal love affair with law is over—until finally and for good, our lifelong certainty that someone is keeping score has run out of steam and collapsed." (*Between Noon and Three* p. 7, Harper & Row, 1982)

"The Reformation was a time when men went blind, staggering drunk because they had discovered, in the dusty basement of late medievalism, a whole cellar full of fifteen-hundred-year-old, two-hundred proof Grace — bottle after bottle of pure distillate of Scripture, one sip of which would convince anyone that God saves us single-handedly. The word of the Gospel—after all those centuries of trying to lift yourself into heaven by worrying about the perfection of your bootstraps—suddenly turned out to be a flat announcement that the saved were home before they started... Grace has to be drunk straight: no water, no ice, and certainly no ginger ale; neither goodness, nor badness, nor the flowers that bloom in the spring of super spirituality could be allowed to enter into the case." (*Ibid.* p. 109)

"What role have I left for religion? None. And I have left none because the Gospel of our Lord and Savior Jesus Christ leaves none. Christianity is not a religion; it is the announcement of the end of religion. Religion consists of all the things (believing, behaving, worshiping, sacrificing) the human race has ever thought it had to do to get right with God. About those things, Christianity has only two comments to make. The first is that none of them ever had the least chance of doing the trick: the blood of bulls and goats can never take away sins (see the Epistle to the Hebrews) and no effort of ours to keep the law of God can ever succeed (see the Epistle to the Romans). The second is that everything religion tried (and failed) to do has been perfectly done, once and for all, by Jesus in his death and resurrection. For Christians, therefore, the entire religion shop has been closed, boarded up, and forgotten. The church is not in the religion business. It never has been and it never will be, in spite of all the ecclesiastical turkeys through two thousand years who have acted as if religion was their stock in trade. The church, instead, is in the Gospel-proclaiming business. It is not here to bring the world the bad news that God will think kindly about us only after we have gone through certain creedal, liturgical, and ethical wickets; it is here to bring the world the Good News that 'while we were yet sinners, Christ died for the ungodly.' It is here, in short, for no religious purpose at all, only to announce the Gospel of free grace." (*Kingdom, Grace, Judgment: Paradox, Outrage, and Vindication in the Parables of Jesus*, Kindle Locations 3222-3232)

Karl Barth:

"...The God of the Gospel is no lonely God, self-sufficient and self-contained. He is no 'absolute' God (in the original sense of absolute, i.e., being detached from everything that is not himself). To be sure, he has no equal beside himself, since and equal would no doubt limit, influence, and determine him. On the other hand, he is not imprisoned by his own majesty, as though he were bound to be no more than the personal (or impersonal) 'wholly other.' ... Just as his oneness consists in the unity of his life as Father, Son, and Holy Spirit, so in relation to the reality distinct from him he is free de jure and de facto to be the

God of man. He exists neither next to man nor merely above him, but rather with him, by him, and most important of all, for him. He is man's God not only as Lord but also as father, brother, friend; and this relationship implies neither a diminution nor in any way a denial, but, instead, a confirmation and display of his divine essence itself." (*Evangelical Theology: An Introduction*, pp. 10-1, Eerdmans, 1992)

"The content of God's Word is his free, undeserved Yes to the whole human race, in spite of all human unreasonableness and corruption." (*Ibid.* p. 79)

"Repentance is not an affair that we can accomplish in our own resources." (*The Holy Spirit and the Christian Life* p. 28, Westminster John Knox Press, 1993)

"God willed from all eternity not to be without man." (*Church Dogmatics* IV.1 p. 104, T&T Clark, 2004)

"Whatever we have to think and say of man, and not only of the Christian man but of man in general, at every point we have to think and say it of his being as man reconciled in Jesus Christ.

We speak of man reconciled in Jesus Christ and therefore of the being which is that of man in Him... The grace of God in which it comes and is made over to us is the grace of Jesus Christ, that is, the grace in which God from all eternity has chosen men (all men) in this One, in which he has bound Himself to man–before man even existed– in this One. He, Jesus Christ, is the One who accomplishes the sovereign act in which God has made true and actual in time the decree of His election by making atonement, in which He has introduced the new being of all men." (*Church Dogmatics* IV.1 p. 91-2, Hendrickson Publishers, 2010)

"Jesus Christ is God's mighty command to open our eyes and to realize that this place is all around us, that we are already in this kingdom, that we have no alternative but to adjust ourselves to it, that we have our being and continuance here and nowhere else. In Him we are already there, we already belong to it. To enter at His command is to realize that in Him we are already inside. ... That is why we use the word direction—we might almost say the advice or hint. It is not a loud and stern and foreign thing, but the quiet and gentle and intimate awakening of children in the Father's house to life in that house." (*Ibid.* p. 99-100)

Jürgen Moltmann:

"Real joy stimulates the soul, makes relationships flourish, makes the heart light and limbs nimble, mobilizes undreamed-of powers, and increases confidence. Genuine happiness lays hold of the person's whole being. In joy, the ecstatic nature of human existence finds its true expression. We are made for joy. We are born for joy." (*The Living God and the Fullness of Life*, p. 97, Westminster John Knox Press, 2015)

"When the crucified Jesus is called the 'image of the invisible God', the meaning is that this is God, and God is like this. God is not greater than he is in this humiliation. God is not more glorious than he is in this self-surrender. God is not more powerful than he is in this helplessness. God is not more divine than he is in this humanity." (*The Crucified God*, p. 205, Fortress Press, 1974)